I WANT TO BE A
HOTEL MANAGER

Written by
Jonathan Reule

Illustration
Caballero Peza Mauricio
&
Caballero Peza Gabriel Fernando

Storyboard
Christiane Tee

UNIBINO
BOOKS

First paperback edition October 2023
ISBN 978-981-18-7877-0

Published by Unibino Pte. Ltd.
9 North Buona Vista Drive, #02-01 Metropolis Tower 1, Singapore 138588

www.unibino.com

Hotels are often great places to stay when we are far from our homes. These places can range from a small comfortable room to a grand suite, large enough to fit an entire family inside. But no matter the type of hotel, one thing is for sure, these places need dedicated hotel managers to help keep them up and running!

Perhaps you've stayed in a hotel before? And perhaps you used the amenities available at those places, like pools, dining halls, and even playgrounds. But did you know it takes quite a lot of work to upkeep such an establishment? There is more work going on than you can imagine at your average hotel, which is why Hotel Managers are so important.

But before we book a reservation in this story, we should first take a step back and have a look at how Hotels originally formed. Do you know why we needed hotels in the first place? Well, long ago, before we built our homes on solid ground, we used to be nomads moving from place to place.

Our homes were often tents we could assemble and disassemble with ease - so that we weren't bound to one single location for very long. This was a nice way of life, but one that became tiring after a while. And that's when we longed to stay put in a single place where we could provide for all our needs without following animals or moving from climate to climate every few months.

It would take us several thousand years before we finally dedicated ourselves to one single location. This was when many ancient empires started to arise in regions such as Mesopotamia, Egypt, and throughout the Indus Valley. But just because we established these great cities to live in, it didn't remove the fact that we still needed to travel.

In fact, international trading and commerce were prominent jobs back in those times. These traders would often travel from city to city, trading food, clothes, pottery, and items considered a luxury, such as copper. Although there were sometimes outposts between cities where traders could stay, they often needed to reach the city centre, which required them to find a place to stay for several days.

For quite some time, these traders would sleep in their own tents or caravans outside these foreign cities while selling their merchandise to willing patrons. Eventually, governments began realising that something needed to be done. They needed traders to bring them items from faraway lands, but these traders, in return, needed lodging to be at their best when selling goods.

This is how some of the first lodgings came about. You see, in the ancient city of Kanesh, a special building was erected to help quarter these traders and merchants from all over the world. But these quarters weren't free. Instead, the traders were required to pay a small tax to the city upon entry, which would then allow them to stay at these special quarters for their short-term lodgings.

As civilisations progressed, though, so did our lodgings. In the ancient Greco-Roman times, several places would offer lodgings to travellers. Hospitals were a common area for a traveller to take a break and recuperate. Another option for traders was to stay at a local Tabernae (taverns), where they could not only get food and drinks but also stay for the night.

For traders who developed strong connections with the locals in those cities, they could also have the option of staying in private homes if their friends were willing to keep them! But we were far from having a proper hotel manager overseeing these establishments' operations. This was often the responsibility of the Tabernae's owner - who was also the cook, cleaner, and bookkeeper!

During the middle ages, it was more common for monasteries and other religious institutions to offer accommodations for travellers. These places were often bare bones, meaning some might not even have proper beds for guests to sleep on.

Another downside was the varied treatment given to the travelers. One person may have had a great experience, while another could have been ignored the entire time. Much of this, sadly, had to do with how people presented themselves at these facilities. If they looked well-dressed, they might receive better treatment than others.

However, there were other forms of short-term lodging that cropped up in the Middle Ages that were different from monasteries. One concept was the guest house, the predecessor to modern hotels. These guest houses could be attached to monasteries or even standalone buildings run as their own independent businesses.

But did you know the oldest guest house was founded in Yamanashi, Japan, in 705 AD? This is what many consider to be the very first hotel, even though it wasn't called a hotel. It had a hot spring attached to the building and several rooms for guests to stay during their trips. What's more interesting is that the same family has owned this hotel for over 52 generations!

Now if we hop ahead to fifteenth-century Europe, we'll find the beginnings of the first modern hotels in what was known as Coaching Inns. The Inns were similar to the Roman tabernae. Only these inns started to attract wealthy clientele, making them lucrative businesses for many owners, which naturally brought lots of competition.

The Inn owners soon started to have more things to do than a single owner could handle. Many Inns had stables where travellers could leave their horses during their stays, which required plenty of work. Rooms had to be made up nicely and furnished to the client's liking. Not to mention food needed to be prepared properly for the guests too!

As you can see, it became almost impossible for the owners to keep guests happy while staying up with the rival inns without assistance from a dedicated manager. But instead of this trend dying down, it only became more prevalent. In no time, luxury hotels began to crop up, creating an entirely different type of experience for travellers.

They were a new concept at first and took some time to catch on, but when they did, their presence exploded across the map! People began taking to the idea of these hotels where they could be catered to while on short stays away from home. To most people, hotels could be a home away from home for a brief time.

This, of course, brings us to the modern day, where hotels are spread all across the globe in nearly every country of the world! But modern hotels are no easy feat to manage. There is plenty of work to be done each and every single day.

Modern hotels have a wide range of offerings between them. Some are boutiques with fewer rooms but more personalised touches. Others are massive structures with thousands of rooms ready to host loads of tourists! There are even uniquely themed hotels - like the Icehotel in Sweden!

But what sort of tasks do Hotel Managers need to do on a regular basis to keep these hotels running smoothly? Most have to juggle multiple roles, such as training new staff or checking the hotel's budget, and even staying ahead of trends to keep their hotel up to date. They can also be found viewing customer feedback reports to see what clients enjoyed about their experience and what things they may have disliked.

In this way, Hotel Managers need to have good interpersonal skills as they will be communicating with not only the staff but also the guests during their working days. They should also be well organised and pay attention to details since they may be required to juggle several things simultaneously.

You may be wondering, at this point, what does it take to become a Hotel Manager? Well, there are a few different routes to choose from, but the most common is by obtaining a degree in hospitality or hotel management before applying for a job in the hotel industry. But this isn't the only option. There are also hotel manager certifications you could obtain, or better yet, get a job at a hotel to gain practical experience.

After that, it's a good idea to figure out what type of hotel you might want to work at and where you would be best suited. Some hotel managers work at quaint bed and breakfasts managing a smaller roster of clients and rooms. While some managers find themselves in giant hotels with thousands of guests checking in and out on a single day!

Why don't we look at some of these options in a little more detail? For example, did you know there are underwater hotels? That's right; there are novelty hotels that are partially or even completely submerged. To manage a hotel like this, there are different things to consider: How will you transport your customers to your hotel still dry? What will you do if the guests want pizzas delivered to their room at night?

How about the world's largest single hotel called the MGM Grand in Las Vegas? How do you think things would be different for a hotel manager there when the building has over 5000 guest rooms? Firstly, you might work alongside several other hotel managers to coordinate everything. Secondly, you could be dealing with a larger staff along with a mound of guest feedback from all the visitors!

What do you think needs to be managed at an eco-hotel? How about a luxury eco-hotel on a private island? In a hotel like this, you may need to be very detailed and careful in how you train staff because everything needs to be environmentally friendly. These types of hotels might attract celebrities and other famous people who want to get away from the world while staying in an eco-friendly resort and they might expect a different level of treatment during their stay.

Can you imagine what goes into managing a bed and breakfast in a quaint and historical town? It would certainly be different from a bustling hotel in Dubai. Perhaps this manager would need to make sure the food sourced for the guests are of the highest quality. Maybe they need to be more hands-on and helpful with the guests about activities outside the hotel.

As you can probably tell, every hotel will have its own set of requirements and responsibilities. But under a strong Hotel Manager's leadership, these hotels can thrive while making for a pleasant experience for their guests.

Now it's up to you to decide whether pursuing a career as a Hotel Manager is right for you. As you can see, hotels have been around for a long time and will remain important in time to come. Will you be ready to lead these establishments into the future? The choice is yours!

My Inspiration

Shubhi Saxena
Founder, Unibino

As a parent in this ever-changing world, it can sometimes feel overwhelming when it comes to our children's futures. New technologies seem to be arising almost every day, and with so many innovations, it creates unique professions which many of us wouldn't have dreamed to be necessary only a few years ago. Which to me is a good thing. Because with so much variety, my children can have the opportunity to pick a career that will fit their personalities and build upon their strengths. As you may imagine, this desire within me to provide my children with the resources they needed to thrive, led me to search out books that would be easy enough for them to understand while teaching them about various professions.

Only, I found that these books were few and far between. Even if I could find a book about a certain profession geared towards young readers, I found them sparse inside and limited to only certain careers that may not fit my children's abilities. This is when I came up with the idea to write my own children's books, teaching them about all the various careers in the modern world. After months of researching different professions and learning more than I ever expected, I quickly realised this was going to be a bigger project than I first anticipated. I dove into the histories of these professions, discovering links to the past, and why these professions were now so important.

Ultimately my goal was to offer my children options, to show them that there is no one set path for everyone. But in this, I stumbled upon something bigger. I wanted to share this with future generations. To share with all children and parents about these careers, to help spark curiosity, and to instil a passion for the future. Everyone has special talents and abilities, and I hope that this series will be able to offer clarity and inspiration to children around the world. Because at the end of the day, it's never too early to start dreaming and never too late to take action. With this, I hope you enjoy this series and that your young ones become the best versions of themselves as they can achieve.